# Discovering Doctrine
## A Personal Bible Study
### For Grades 7–12

by
Sonya Shafer

Discovering Doctrine: A Personal Bible Study
© 2006, Sonya Shafer

All rights reserved. No part of this work may be reproduced or distributed in any form by any means—graphic, electronic, or mechanical, including photocopying, recording, taping, or storing in information storage and retrieval systems—without written permission from the publisher.

> If you are a parent or teacher you may duplicate pages for yourself and students in your immediate household or classroom. Please do not duplicate pages for friends, relatives outside your immediate household, or other teachers' students.

Published by
Simply Charlotte Mason, LLC
P.O. Box 892
Grayson, Georgia 30017-0892

ISBN 978-1-61634-023-0

www.SimplyCharlotteMason.com

# Contents

How to Use This Study................................5

The Bible (Bibliology)................................7

God (Theology Proper)..............................19

Jesus Christ (Christology)...........................31

Holy Spirit (Pneumatology)........................43

Man (Anthropology)................................55

Sin (Hamartiology)..................................67

Salvation (Soteriology)..............................79

Angels (Angelology).................................91

The Church (Ecclesiology).........................103

Future Events (Eschatology)......................115

# How to Use This Study

## Step One: Look for Doctrine Discoveries

"Doctrine" means "teaching." As you read the Bible during your regular school work, church attendance, or personal devotions in the coming months, watch for what it teaches about these ten main doctrines.

- The Bible (Bibliology) Pg. 7
- God (Theology Proper) Pg. 19
- Jesus Christ (Christology) Pg. 31
- Holy Spirit (Pneumatology) Pg. 43
- Man (Anthropology) Pg. 55
- Sin (Hamartiology) Pg. 67
- Salvation (Soteriology) Pg. 79
- Angels (Angelology) Pg. 91
- Church (Ecclesiology) Pg. 103
- Future Events (Eschatology) Pg. 115

When you discover a teaching that falls into one of those categories, record that statement on a page in the corresponding doctrine's section. Be sure to record the Scripture reference where you find each statement.

For example, if you began reading in Genesis 1 you would discover a doctrine teaching in verse 1 about God. You could record "In the beginning God created the heaven and the earth—Genesis 1:1" as the first entry in your notebook in the doctrine of God section (Theology Proper).

As you continued reading, you would discover a teaching about the Holy Spirit in verse 2 to record in the doctrine of the Holy Spirit section (Pneumatology).

From verses 3–25 you could record all the specific things that God created, or you could simply summarize that first chapter of Genesis by recording "God is the creator of everything—Genesis 1:1–25" in the Theology Proper section. It's your notebook; you decide what to write.

Verse 27 could be recorded in the doctrine of Man section (Anthropology) since it teaches us that mankind is made in the image of God.

Now, not every verse will contain a teaching about a doctrine. For example, many verses describe what someone did or give Christian-living instructions, but they don't necessarily teach us about what man is like or what God is like. It might be helpful to read and search for teachings together with your parent for the first few chapters until you get the hang of what to record and what doesn't necessarily need to be recorded. Some guiding questions are given in each section to give you an idea of what kinds of teachings to look for and record.

When the passage does contain a teaching, you determine in which section you want to record it. Some teachings apply to more than one doctrine. Or you could record the teaching under all applicable doctrine sections; that's fine. The main point is to get into the Word and organize what it teaches about these key doctrines so you can accomplish Step Two.

## Step Two: Write Your Personal Doctrinal Statement

After you have read the Bible and organized its teachings under the ten main doctrines, you are ready to prepare a personal doctrinal statement—What do you believe about those doctrines?

Going through your *Discovering Doctrine* notebook one subject at a time, review all the teachings you have recorded, along with their corresponding Scriptures, and write a narration, or essay, that organizes and summarizes that doctrine. When you have completed one doctrine, move on to the next until you have ten summaries that detail what you believe.

As you can see, this study is no quick assignment; however, it is a vitally important one! Ideally, you should take several years to read the entire Bible, record its teachings about each doctrine, then organize and summarize your findings in written form. We recommend you begin this process in seventh grade and continue it through high school, using twelfth grade to review and write the ten narrations that will comprise your personal doctrinal statement. If you are beginning this study after seventh grade, don't worry about it, but be aware that you may need to put in some significant time to make sure you get all the way through the Bible and still have time to write your ten summaries.

Make the commitment now to complete this project. If you are faithful to keep an eye open for doctrine discoveries every time you read the Bible, you will develop an important life-long habit that will serve you well. And if you are diligent to record and organize those discoveries over the coming months, you will build for yourself a wonderful tool that will help you to stand strong, knowing what you believe and why.

No other subject in your education is as important as this one! Pray for guidance as you read and seek to understand the truth about the Bible, God, Jesus Christ, the Holy Spirit, Man, Sin, Salvation, Angels, the Church, and Future Events.

May God bless you in your study of His Word!

# The Bible

## Bibliology

- What does the Bible claim about itself?

- What other words are used to refer to God's Word?

- What descriptions are given of God's Word?

- What did Jesus say about the Bible?

- What did other people say about the Bible?

# The Bible *Bibliology*

• What does the Bible claim about itself? • What other words are used to refer to God's Word? • What descriptions are given of God's Word? • What did Jesus say about the Bible? • What did other people say about the Bible? • What does the Bible claim about itself? • What other words are used to refer to God's Word? • What descriptions are given of God's Word? • What did Jesus say about the Bible? • What did other people say about the Bible? • What does the Bible claim about itself? • What other words are used to refer to God's Word?

# The Bible
## *Bibliology*

- What does the Bible claim about itself? • What other words are used to refer to God's Word? • What descriptions are given of God's Word? • What did Jesus say about the Bible? • What did other people say about the Bible? • What does the Bible claim about itself? • What other words are used to refer to God's Word? • What descriptions are given of God's Word? • What did Jesus say about the Bible? • What did other people say about the Bible? • What does the Bible claim about itself? • What other words are used to refer to God's Word? • What descriptions are given

# The Bible *Bibliology*

• What does the Bible claim about itself? • What other words are used to refer to God's Word? • What descriptions are given of God's Word? • What did Jesus say about the Bible? • What did other people say about the Bible? • What does the Bible claim about itself? • What other words are used to refer to God's Word? • What descriptions are given of God's Word? • What did Jesus say about the Bible? • What did other people say about the Bible? • What does the Bible claim about itself? • What other words are used to refer to God's Word?

# The Bible
## Bibliology

*Margin prompts (repeating around the page):* What does the Bible claim about itself? • What other words are used to refer to God's Word? • What descriptions are given of God's Word? • What did Jesus say about the Bible? • What did other people say about the Bible?

# The Bible
## *Bibliology*

• What does the Bible claim about itself? • What other words are used to refer to God's Word? • What descriptions are given of God's Word? • What did Jesus say about the Bible? • What did other people say about the Bible? • What does the Bible claim about itself? • What other words are used to refer to God's Word? • What descriptions are given of God's Word? • What did Jesus say about the Bible? • What did other people say about the Bible? • What does the Bible claim about itself? • What other words are used to refer to God's Word?

# The Bible
## *Bibliology*

- What does the Bible claim about itself? • What other words are used to refer to God's Word? • What descriptions are given of God's Word? • What did Jesus say about the Bible? • What did other people say about the Bible? • What does the Bible claim about itself? • What other words are used to refer to God's Word? • What descriptions are given of God's Word? • What did Jesus say about the Bible? • What did other people say about the Bible? • What does the Bible claim about itself? • What other words are used to refer to God's Word? • What descriptions are given

# The Bible
## *Bibliology*

- What does the Bible claim about itself?
- What other words are used to refer to God's Word?
- What descriptions are given of God's Word?
- What did Jesus say about the Bible?
- What did other people say about the Bible?

# The Bible
## Bibliology

- What does the Bible claim about itself? • What other words are used to refer to God's Word? • What descriptions are given of God's Word? • What did Jesus say about the Bible? • What did other people say about the Bible? • What does the Bible claim about itself? • What other words are used to refer to God's Word? • What descriptions are given of God's Word? • What did Jesus say about the Bible? • What did other people say about the Bible? • What does the Bible claim about itself? • What other words are used to refer to God's Word? • What descriptions are given

# The Bible
## Bibliology

- What does the Bible claim about itself? • What other words are used to refer to God's Word? • What descriptions are given of God's Word? • What did Jesus say about the Bible? • What did other people say about the Bible? • What does the Bible claim about itself? • What other words are used to refer to God's Word? • What descriptions are given of God's Word? • What did Jesus say about the Bible? • What did other people say about the Bible? • What does the Bible claim about itself? • What other words are used to refer to God's Word? • What descriptions are given

# The Bible
## Bibliology

*What does the Bible claim about itself? • What other words are used to refer to God's Word? • What descriptions are given of God's Word? • What did Jesus say about the Bible? • What did other people say about the Bible? • What does the Bible claim about itself? • What other words are used to refer to God's Word? • What did Jesus say about the Bible? • What did other people say about the Bible? • What does the Bible claim about itself? • What other words are used to refer to God's Word? • What descriptions are given*

# God: Theology Proper

- What is God like?

- How has God revealed Himself to mankind?

- What are God's characteristics (attributes)?

- What does God call Himself?

- How do we know God exists?

# God Theology Proper

God is the creator genesis 1
after God created everything he rested on
the seventh day God numbered the stars
god is three in one Father, Son and Holy
Spirit. God created man in his own image
God made the tree of Life  God is eternal

# God
## Theology Proper

- What is God like? • How has God revealed Himself to mankind? • What are God's characteristics (attributes)? • What does God call Himself? • How do we know God exists?

# God
## Theology Proper

- What is God like? • How has God revealed Himself to mankind? • What are God's characteristics (attributes)? • What does God call Himself? • How do we know God exists? • What is God like? • How has God revealed Himself to mankind? • What are God's characteristics (attributes)? • What does God call Himself? • How do we know God exists?

# God
## Theology Proper

_Margin questions: What is God like? • How has God revealed Himself to mankind? • What are God's characteristics (attributes)? • What does God call Himself? • How do we know God exists?_

# God
## Theology Proper

• What is God like? • How has God revealed Himself to mankind? • What are God's characteristics (attributes)? • What does God call Himself? • How do we know God exists? • What is God like? • How has God revealed Himself to mankind? • What are God's characteristics (attributes)? • What does God call Himself? • How do we know God exists?

# God
## *Theology Proper*

- What is God like? • How has God revealed Himself to mankind? • What are God's characteristics (attributes)? • What does God call Himself? • How do we know God exists?

# God
## Theology Proper

- What is God like? • How has God revealed Himself to mankind? • What are God's characteristics (attributes)? • What does God call Himself? • How do we know God exists?

_____
_____
_____
_____
_____
_____
_____
_____
_____
_____
_____
_____
_____
_____
_____
_____
_____
_____
_____
_____
_____
_____
_____
_____
_____
_____
_____
_____

God like? • How has God revealed Himself to mankind? • What are God's characteristics (attributes)? • What does God call Himself? • How do we know God

# God
## Theology Proper

- What is God like?
- How has God revealed Himself to mankind?
- What are God's characteristics (attributes)?
- What does God call Himself?
- How do we know God exists?

# God
## Theology Proper

- What is God like? • How has God revealed Himself to mankind? • What are God's characteristics (attributes)? • What does God call Himself? • How do we know God exists?

# God
## Theology Proper

*Margin prompts (repeated on all four sides):* What is God like? • How has God revealed Himself to mankind? • What are God's characteristics (attributes)? • What does God call Himself? • How do we know God exists?

# Jesus Christ
## *Christology*

- Is Jesus God?

- Is Jesus man?

- What did Jesus claim about Himself?

- What did Jesus do during His earthly life?

- What does the Bible say about Jesus' death, resurrection, and ascension?

- What is Jesus' present ministry?

# Jesus Christ *Christology*

• Is Jesus God? • Is Jesus man? • What did Jesus claim about Himself? • What did Jesus do during His earthly life? • What does the Bible say about Jesus' death, resurrection, and ascension?

What is Jesus' present ministry? • Is Jesus God? • Is Jesus man? • What did Jesus claim about Himself? • What did Jesus do during His earthly life? • What does the Bible say about Jesus' death, resurrection, and ascension? • Is Jesus God? • Is Jesus man? • What did Jesus claim about Himself? • What did Jesus do during His earthly life?

# Jesus Christ
## *Christology*

- Is Jesus God? • Is Jesus man? • What did Jesus claim about Himself? • What did Jesus do during His earthly life? • What does the Bible say about Jesus' death, resurrection, and ascension?

- What did Jesus do during His earthly life? • What did Jesus claim about Himself? • Is Jesus man? • Is Jesus God? • Bible say about Jesus' death, resurrection, and ascension?

What is Jesus' present ministry? • Is Jesus God? • Is Jesus man? • What did Jesus claim about Himself? • What did Jesus do during His earthly life • What does the

*www.SimplyCharlotteMason.com* — Discovering Doctrine, 33

# Jesus Christ
## *Christology*

• Is Jesus God? • Is Jesus man? • What did Jesus claim about Himself? • What did Jesus do during His earthly life? • What does the Bible say about Jesus' death, resurrection, and ascension?

What is Jesus' present ministry? • Is Jesus God? • Is Jesus man? • What did Jesus claim about Himself? • What did Jesus do during His earthly life? • What does the Bible say about Jesus' death, resurrection, and ascension? • Is Jesus God? • Is Jesus man? • What did Jesus claim about Himself? • What did Jesus do during His earthly life?

# Jesus Christ *Christology*

• Is Jesus God? • Is Jesus man? • What did Jesus claim about Himself? • What did Jesus do during His earthly life? • What does the Bible say about Jesus' death, resurrection, and ascension?

What is Jesus' present ministry? • Is Jesus God? • Is Jesus man? • What did Jesus claim about Himself? • What did Jesus do during His earthly life? • What does the Bible say about Jesus' death, resurrection, and ascension? • Is Jesus God? • Is Jesus man? • What did Jesus claim about Himself? • What did Jesus do during His earthly life?

# Jesus Christ
## *Christology*

- Is Jesus God? • Is Jesus man? • What did Jesus claim about Himself? • What did Jesus do during His earthly life? • What does the Bible say about Jesus' death, resurrection, and ascension?

_____
_____
_____
_____
_____
_____
_____
_____
_____
_____
_____
_____
_____
_____
_____
_____
_____
_____
_____
_____
_____
_____
_____
_____
_____
_____
_____
_____
_____
_____
_____

What is Jesus' present ministry? • Is Jesus God? • Is Jesus man? • What did Jesus claim about Himself? • What did Jesus do during His earthly life? • What does the

# Jesus Christ
# *Christology*

• Is Jesus God? • Is Jesus man? • What did Jesus claim about Himself? • What did Jesus do during His earthly life? • What does the Bible say about Jesus' death, resurrection, and ascension?

What is Jesus' present ministry? • Is Jesus God? • Is Jesus man? • What did Jesus claim about Himself? • What did Jesus do during His earthly life? • What does the Bible say about Jesus' death, resurrection, and ascension?

• Is Jesus God? • Is Jesus man? • What did Jesus claim about Himself? • What did Jesus do during His earthly life?

# Jesus Christ
## *Christology*

- Is Jesus God? • Is Jesus man? • What did Jesus claim about Himself? • What did Jesus do during His earthly life? • What does the Bible say about Jesus' death, resurrection, and ascension?

_____
_____
_____
_____
_____
_____
_____
_____
_____
_____
_____
_____
_____
_____
_____
_____
_____
_____
_____
_____
_____
_____
_____
_____
_____
_____
_____
_____
_____

What is Jesus' present ministry? • Is Jesus God? • Is Jesus man? • What did Jesus claim about Himself? • What did Jesus do during His earthly life? • What does the

# Jesus Christ
## *Christology*

- Is Jesus God? • Is Jesus man? • What did Jesus claim about Himself? • What did Jesus do during His earthly life? • What does the Bible say about Jesus' death, resurrection, and ascension? • Is Jesus God? • Is Jesus man? • What did Jesus claim about Himself? • What did Jesus do during His earthly life?

_____
_____
_____
_____
_____
_____
_____
_____
_____
_____
_____
_____
_____
_____
_____
_____
_____
_____
_____
_____
_____
_____
_____
_____
_____
_____
_____
_____
_____
_____

What is Jesus' present ministry? • Is Jesus God? • Is Jesus man? • What did Jesus claim about Himself? • What did Jesus do during His earthly life? • What does the

# Jesus Christ
## *Christology*

- Is Jesus God? • Is Jesus man? • What did Jesus claim about Himself? • What did Jesus do during His earthly life? • What does the Bible say about Jesus' death, resurrection, and ascension? • Is Jesus God? • Is Jesus man? • What did Jesus claim about Himself? • What did Jesus do during His earthly life? • What does the Bible say about Jesus' death, resurrection, and ascension? • What is Jesus' present ministry? • Is Jesus God? • Is Jesus man? • What did Jesus claim about Himself? • What did Jesus do during His earthly life? • What does the

# Jesus Christ
## *Christology*

• Is Jesus God? • Is Jesus man? • What did Jesus claim about Himself? • What did Jesus do during His earthly life? • What does the Bible say about Jesus' death, resurrection, and ascension?

What is Jesus' present ministry? • Is Jesus God? • Is Jesus man? • What did Jesus claim about Himself? • What did Jesus do during His earthly life? • What does the Bible say about Jesus' death, resurrection, and ascension? • Is Jesus God? • Is Jesus man? • What did Jesus claim about Himself? • What did Jesus do during His earthly life?

# Holy Spirit
## *Pneumatology*

- What is the Holy Spirit like?

- What are His characteristics (attributes)?

- What is the Holy Spirit's work (ministries)?

# Holy Spirit
## *Pneumatology*

• What is the Holy Spirit like? • What are His characteristics (attributes)? • What is the Holy Spirit's work (ministries)? • What is the Holy Spirit like? • What are His characteristics (attributes)? • What is the Holy Spirit's work (ministries)? • What is the Holy Spirit like? • What are His characteristics (attributes)? • What is the Holy Spirit's work (ministries) • What is the Holy Spirit like? • What are His characteristics (attributes)? • What is the Holy

# Holy Spirit
## Pneumatology

# Holy Spirit
## *Pneumatology*

• What is the Holy Spirit like? • What are His characteristics (attributes)? • What is the Holy Spirit's work (ministries)? • What is the Holy Spirit like? • What are His characteristics (attributes)? • What is the Holy Spirit's work (ministries)? • What is the Holy Spirit like? • What are His characteristics (attributes)? • What is the Holy Spirit's work (ministries)? • What is the Holy Spirit like? • What are His characteristics (attributes)? • What is the Holy Spirit's work (ministries) • What is the Holy Spirit like? • What are His characteristics (attributes)? • What is the Holy

# Holy Spirit
## *Pneumatology*

• What is the Holy Spirit like? • What are His characteristics (attributes)? • What is the Holy Spirit's work (ministries)? • What is the Holy Spirit like? • What are His characteristics (attributes)? • What is the Holy Spirit's work (ministries) • What is the Holy Spirit like? • What are His characteristics (attributes)? • What is the Holy Spirit's work (ministries)? • What is the Holy Spirit like? • What are His characteristics (attributes)? • What is the Holy Spirit's work (ministries)? • What is the Holy Spirit like? • What are His characteristics

*www.SimplyCharlotteMason.com* — Discovering Doctrine, 47

# Holy Spirit
## *Pneumatology*

*Margin prompts:* • What is the Holy Spirit like? • What are His characteristics (attributes)? • What is the Holy Spirit's work (ministries)?

# Holy Spirit
## *Pneumatology*

Border text (repeating): • What is the Holy Spirit like? • What are His characteristics (attributes)? • What is the Holy Spirit's work (ministries)?

# Holy Spirit
## *Pneumatology*

*Margin prompts (repeating):* • What is the Holy Spirit like? • What are His characteristics (attributes)? • What is the Holy Spirit's work (ministries)?

# Holy Spirit
## *Pneumatology*

• What is the Holy Spirit like? • What are His characteristics (attributes)? • What is the Holy Spirit's work (ministries)? • What is the Holy Spirit like? • What are His characteristics (attributes)? • What is the Holy Spirit's work (ministries)? • What is the Holy Spirit like? • What are His characteristics (attributes)? • What is the Holy Spirit's work (ministries) • What is the Holy Spirit like? • What are His characteristics (attributes)? • What is the Holy

# Holy Spirit
## Pneumatology

*Margin prompts (repeating):* • What is the Holy Spirit like? • What are His characteristics (attributes)? • What is the Holy Spirit's work (ministries)?

# Holy Spirit
## *Pneumatology*

• What is the Holy Spirit like? • What are His characteristics (attributes)? • What is the Holy Spirit's work (ministries)? • What is the Holy Spirit like? • What are His characteristics (attributes)? • What is the Holy Spirit's work (ministries)? • What is the Holy Spirit like? • What are His characteristics (attributes)? • What is the Holy Spirit's work (ministries)? • What is the Holy Spirit like? • What are His characteristics (attributes)? • What is the Holy Spirit's work (ministries)? • What is the Holy Spirit like? • What are His characteristics (attributes)? • What is the Holy Spirit's work (ministries) • What is the Holy Spirit like? • What are His characteristics (attributes)? • What is the Holy

# Man
## Anthropology

- How did man come into existence?

- What are the various parts of man: material and immaterial?

- What are man's characteristics?

- What is man responsible for?

- What is man's current spiritual condition and will it get better or worse?

# Man
## Anthropology

man is made in Gods image

# Man
## Anthropology

*How did man come into existence? • What are the various parts of man: material and immaterial? • What are man's characteristics? • What is man responsible for? • What is man's current spiritual condition and will it get better or worse? • How did man come into existence? • What is man's current spiritual condition and will it get better or worse? • How did man come into existence? • What are the various parts of man: material and immaterial? • What are man's characteristics? • What is man responsible for? • What is man's current spiritual condition and will it get better or worse? • How did man come into existence? • What are the various parts of man: material and immaterial? • What are*

# Man
## Anthropology

*Margin questions:* How did man come into existence? • What are the various parts of man: material and immaterial? • What are man's characteristics? • What is man responsible for? • What is man's current spiritual condition and will it get better or worse?

# Man
## Anthropology

*Border questions:* How did man come into existence? • What are the various parts of man: material and immaterial? • What are man's characteristics? • What is man responsible for? • What is man's current spiritual condition and will it get better or worse?

# Man Anthropology

_____

*Side margins (questions):* How did man come into existence? • What are the various parts of man: material and immaterial? • What are man's characteristics? • What is man responsible for? • What is man's current spiritual condition and will it get better or worse? • How did man come into existence? • What are the various parts of man: material and immaterial? • What are

# Man
# Anthropology

*Side margin questions:* How did man come into existence? • What are the various parts of man: material and immaterial? • What are man's characteristics? • What is man responsible for? • What is man's current spiritual condition and will it get better or worse? • How did man come into existence? • What is man's current spiritual condition and will it get better or worse? • What is man responsible for? • What are man's characteristics? • What are the various parts of man: material and immaterial? • How did man come into existence? • spiritual condition and will it get better or worse? • How did man come into existence? • What are the various parts of man: material and immaterial? • What are

# Man
## Anthropology

- How did man come into existence? • What are the various parts of man: material and immaterial? • What are man's characteristics? • What is man responsible for? • What is man's current spiritual condition and will it get better or worse? • How did man come into existence? • What is man responsible for? • What is man's characteristics? • What are man's characteristics? • What is man responsible for? • What is man's current spiritual condition and will it get better or worse? • How did man come into existence? • What are the various parts of man: material and immaterial? • What are

# Man
## Anthropology

- How did man come into existence?
- What are the various parts of man: material and immaterial?
- What are man's characteristics?
- What is man responsible for?
- What is man's current spiritual condition and will it get better or worse?

# Man
## Anthropology

*Side margin questions:* How did man come into existence? • What are the various parts of man: material and immaterial? • What are man's characteristics? • What is man responsible for? • What is man's current spiritual condition and will it get better or worse?

*Discovering Doctrine, 64*

# Man
## Anthropology

*Margin questions:* How did man come into existence? • What are the various parts of man: material and immaterial? • What are man's characteristics? • What is man responsible for? • What is man's current spiritual condition and will it get better or worse?

# Sin
## *Hamartiology*

- What is sin?

- What other words are used for "sin"?

- How did sin come into existence?

- What are the results of sin?

- Who has sinned?

- How can a person deal with sin?

# Sin
## Hamartiology

• What is sin? • What other words are used for "sin"? • How did sin come into existence? • What are the results of sin? • Who has sinned? • How can a person deal with sin? •

_____
_____
_____
_____
_____
_____
_____
_____
_____
_____
_____
_____
_____
_____
_____
_____
_____
_____
_____
_____
_____
_____
_____
_____
_____
_____
_____
_____
_____

• What other words are used for "sin"? • How did sin come into existence? • What are the results of sin? • Who has sinned? • How can a person deal with sin? •

# Sin
## Hamartiology

*Margin questions (repeated on all four sides):* What is sin? • What other words are used for "sin"? • How did sin come into existence? • What are the results of sin? • Who has sinned? • How can a person deal with sin?

# Sin
## Hamartiology

- What other words are used for "sin"? • How did sin come into existence? • What are the results of sin? • Who has sinned? • How can a person deal with sin? •

# Sin
## *Hamartiology*

*Margin prompts:* What is sin? • What other words are used for "sin"? • How did sin come into existence? • What are the results of sin? • Who has sinned? • How can a person deal with sin?

# Sin
## *Hamartiology*

*What is sin? • What other words are used for "sin"? • How did sin come into existence? • What are the results of sin? • Who has sinned? • How can a person deal with sin?*

# Sin
# *Hamartiology*

- What is sin? • What other words are used for "sin"? • How did sin come into existence? • What are the results of sin? • Who has sinned? • How can a person deal with sin? • What is sin?

- What is sin? • What other words are used for "sin"? • How did sin come into existence? • What are the results of sin? • Who has sinned? • How can a person deal with sin? • What is sin?

• What other words are used for "sin"? • How did sin come into existence? • What are the results of sin? • Who has sinned? • How can a person deal with sin? •

# Sin
## *Hamartiology*

*Margin prompts:* • What is sin? • What other words are used for "sin"? • How did sin come into existence? • What are the results of sin? • Who has sinned? • How can a person deal with sin?

# Sin
## Hamartiology

*Margin prompts (repeated on all four sides):* • What is sin? • What other words are used for "sin"? • How did sin come into existence? • What are the results of sin? • Who has sinned? • How can a person deal with sin?

# Sin
## Hamartiology

• What is sin? • What other words are used for "sin"? • How did sin come into existence? • What are the results of sin? • Who has sinned? • How can a person deal with sin? •

# Sin
## Hamartiology

*What is sin? • What other words are used for "sin"? • How did sin come into existence? • What are the results of sin? • Who has sinned? • How can a person deal with sin?*

# Salvation
## *Soteriology*

- What is God's plan to save people from sin?

- Who can be saved?

- What are the benefits of salvation?

- What are the requirements for salvation?

- What key words are used in regard to salvation and what do those words mean?

- How can a person know he is saved?

# Salvation
## Soteriology

*Margin questions:* What is God's plan to save people from sin? • Who can be saved? • What are the benefits of salvation? • What are the requirements for salvation? • What key words are used in regard to salvation and what do those words mean? • How can a person know he is saved?

Discovering Doctrine, 80

# Salvation
## *Soteriology*

- What is God's plan to save people from sin?
- Who can be saved?
- What are the benefits of salvation?
- What are the requirements for salvation?
- What key words are used in regard to salvation and what do those words mean?
- How can a person know he is saved?

# Salvation
## Soteriology

*Margin prompts:* What is God's plan to save people from sin? • Who can be saved? • What are the benefits of salvation? • What are the requirements for salvation? • What key words are used in regard to salvation and what do those words mean? • How can a person know he is saved?

# Salvation
## Soteriology

*Side margin questions:* What is God's plan to save people from sin? • Who can be saved? • What are the benefits of salvation? • What are the requirements for salvation? • What key words are used in regard to salvation and what do those words mean? • How can a person know he is saved?

# Salvation
## *Soteriology*

*Margin questions (left, top, right, bottom):* What is God's plan to save people from sin? • Who can be saved? • What are the benefits of salvation? • What are the requirements for salvation? • What key words are used in regard to salvation and what do those words mean? • How can a person know he is saved?

# Salvation
## *Soteriology*

*Side margin questions:* What is God's plan to save people from sin? • Who can be saved? • What are the benefits of salvation? • What are the requirements for salvation? • What key words are used in regard to salvation and what do those words mean? • How can a person know he is saved?

# Salvation
## *Soteriology*

Margin questions: What is God's plan to save people from sin? • Who can be saved? • What are the benefits of salvation? • What are the requirements for salvation? • What key words are used in regard to salvation and what do those words mean? • How can a person know he is saved?

# Salvation
## Soteriology

*Margin questions:* What is God's plan to save people from sin? • Who can be saved? • What are the benefits of salvation? • What are the requirements for salvation? • What key words are used in regard to salvation and what do those words mean? • How can a person know he is saved?

# Salvation
## Soteriology

*Discovering Doctrine, 88*

*Margin questions:* What is God's plan to save people from sin? • Who can be saved? • What are the benefits of salvation? • What are the requirements for salvation? • What key words are used in regard to salvation and what do those words mean? • How can a person know he is saved?

# Salvation
## Soteriology

- What is God's plan to save people from sin?
- Who can be saved?
- What are the benefits of salvation?
- What are the requirements for salvation?
- What key words are used in regard to salvation and what do those words mean?
- How can a person know he is saved?

# Angels
## Angelology

- Where did angels come from?
- What are angels like?
- What names are mentioned for angels?
- What is the angels' work (ministries)?
- What are demons?
- What work do demons do?
- Who is Satan?
- What work does Satan do?
- What limits are put on Satan's and demons' work?

# Angels
## Angelology

- Where did angels come from? • What are angels like? • What names are mentioned for angels? • What is the angels' work (ministries)? • What are demons? • What work do demons do?

- Who is Satan? • What work does Satan do? • What work do demons do? • What are demons? • What is the angels' work (ministries)? • What names are mentioned for angels?

- Who is Satan? • What work does Satan do? • What limits are put on Satan's and demons' work? • Where did angels come from? • What are angels like?

# Angels

*Angelology*

• Where did angels come from? • What are angels like? • What names are mentioned for angels? • What is the angels' work (ministries)? • What are demons? • What work do demons do?

• Who is Satan? • What work does Satan do? • What limits are put on Satan's and demons' work? • Where did angels come from? • What are angels like? •

What names are mentioned for angels? • What is the angels' work (ministries)? • What are demons? • What work do demons do? • Who is Satan? • What work does Satan do?

# Angels
## Angelology

- Where did angels come from? • What are angels like? • What names are mentioned for angels? • What is the angels' work (ministries)? • What are demons? • What work do demons do?

- Who is Satan? • What work does Satan do? • What are demons? • What work do demons do? • What is the angels' work (ministries)? • What names are mentioned for angels? •

- Who is Satan? • What work does Satan do? • What limits are put on Satan's and demons' work? • Where did angels come from? • What are angels like? •

*Discovering Doctrine, 94*  *www.SimplyCharlotteMason.com*

# Angels

*Angelology*

• Where did angels come from? • What are angels like? • What names are mentioned for angels? • What is the angels' work (ministries)? • What are demons? • What work do demons do?

What names are mentioned for angels? • What is the angels' work (ministries)? • What are demons? • What work do demons do? • Who is Satan? • What work does Satan do?

• Who is Satan? • What work does Satan do? • What limits are put on Satan's and demons' work? • Where did angels come from? • What are angels like? •

# Angels
## Angelology

- Where did angels come from? • What are angels like? • What names are mentioned for angels? • What is the angels' work (ministries)? • What are demons? • What work do demons do?

- Who is Satan? • What work does Satan do? • What limits are put on Satan's and demons' work? • Where did angels come from? • What are angels like? •

- What names are mentioned for angels? • What is the angels' work (ministries)? • What are demons? • What work do demons do? • Who is Satan? • What work does Satan do?

# Angels
## Angelology

- Where did angels come from? • What are angels like? • What names are mentioned for angels? • What is the angels' work (ministries)? • What are demons? • What work do demons do?

- What work does Satan do? • Who is Satan? • What work do demons do? • What are demons? • What is the angels' work (ministries)? • What names are mentioned for angels?

- Who is Satan? • What work does Satan do? • What limits are put on Satan's and demons' work? • Where did angels come from? • What are angels like?

# Angels
## Angelology

- Where did angels come from? • What are angels like? • What names are mentioned for angels? • What is the angels' work (ministries)? • What are demons? • What work do demons do?

- Who is Satan? • What work does Satan do? • What work do demons do? • What are demons? • What work do the angels' ministries? • What names are mentioned for angels?

- Who is Satan? • What work does Satan do? • What limits are put on Satan's and demons' work? • Where did angels come from? • What are angels like? •

# Angels
## Angelology

- Where did angels come from? • What are angels like? • What names are mentioned for angels? • What is the angels' work (ministries)? • What are demons? • What work do demons do?

- Who is Satan? • What work does Satan do? • What limits are put on Satan's and demons' work? • Where did angels come from? • What are angels like? •

- What work does Satan do? • Who is Satan? • What work do demons do? • What are demons? • What is the angels' work (ministries)? • What names are mentioned for angels?

# Angels

## *Angelology*

• Where did angels come from? • What are angels like? • What names are mentioned for angels? • What is the angels' work (ministries)? • What are demons? • What work do demons do?

What names are mentioned for angels? • What is the angels' work (ministries)? • What are demons? • What work do demons do? • Who is Satan? • What work does Satan do?

• Who is Satan? • What work does Satan do? • What limits are put on Satan's and demons' work? • Where did angels come from? • What are angels like? •

# Angels
## Angelology

- Where did angels come from? • What are angels like? • What names are mentioned for angels? • What is the angels' work (ministries)? • What are demons? • What work do demons do?

- What work does Satan do? • Who is Satan? • What work do demons do? • What are demons? • What is the angels' work (ministries)? • What names are mentioned for angels? •

- Who is Satan? • What work does Satan do? • What limits are put on Satan's and demons' work? • Where did angels come from? • What are angels like? •

# The Church
## Ecclesiology

- What is the church?

- What is the purpose of the church?

- What work (ministries) should the church do?

- What other names are given for "the church"?

- What are the qualifications for the church's leaders?

# The Church
## Ecclesiology

*What is the church? • What is the purpose of the church? • What work (ministries) should the church do? • What other names are given for "the church"? • What are the qualifications for the church's leaders? • What is the church? • What is the purpose of the church? • What work (ministries) should the church do? • What other names are given for "the church"? • What are the qualifications for the church's leaders? • What is the church? • What is the purpose of the church? • What work (ministries) should the church do? • What other names are given for "the church"? • What are the qualifications for the church's leaders?*

# The Church
## *Ecclesiology*

• What is the church? • What is the purpose of the church? • What work (ministries) should the church do? • What other names are given for "the church"? • What are the qualifications for the church's leaders? • What is the church? • What is the purpose of the church? • What work (ministries) should the church do?

# The Church
## *Ecclesiology*

• What is the church? • What is the purpose of the church? • What work (ministries) should the church do? • What other names are given for "the church"? • What are the qualifications for the church's leaders? • What is the church? • What is the purpose of the church? • What work (ministries) should the church do?

# The Church
## *Ecclesiology*

- What is the church? • What is the purpose of the church? • What work (ministries) should the church do? • What other names are given for "the church"? • What are the qualifications for the church's leaders? • What is the church? • What is the purpose of the church? • What work (ministries) should the church do? • What other names are given for "the church"? • What are the qualifications for the church's leaders? • What is the church? • What is the purpose of the church? • What work (ministries) should the church do? • What other names are given

# The Church
## Ecclesiology

- What is the church? • What is the purpose of the church? • What work (ministries) should the church do? • What other names are given for "the church"? • What are the qualifications for the church's leaders? • What is the church? • What is the purpose of the church? • What work (ministries) should the church do? • What other names are given for "the church"? • What are the qualifications for the church's leaders? • What is the church? • What is the purpose of the church? • What work (ministries) should the church do? • What other names are given for the church's leaders? • What is the church? • What is the purpose of the church? • What work (ministries) should the church do? • What other names are given

# The Church
## *Ecclesiology*

- What is the church? • What is the purpose of the church? • What work (ministries) should the church do? • What other names are given for "the church"? • What are the qualifications for the church's leaders? • What is the church? • What is the purpose of the church? • What work (ministries) should the church do? • What other names are given for "the church"? • What are the qualifications for the church's leaders? • What is the church? • What is the purpose of the church? • What work (ministries) should the church do? • What other names are given

# The Church
## *Ecclesiology*

*Margin prompts:* What is the church? • What is the purpose of the church? • What work (ministries) should the church do? • What other names are given for "the church"? • What are the qualifications for the church's leaders?

# The Church

## *Ecclesiology*

• What is the church? • What is the purpose of the church? • What work (ministries) should the church do? • What other names are given for "the church"? • What are the qualifications

for the church's leaders? • What is the church? • What is the purpose of the church? • What work (ministries) should the church do? • What other names are given

for "the church"? • What are the qualifications for the church's leaders? • What is the church? • What is the purpose of the church? • What work (ministries) should the church do?

# The Church
## *Ecclesiology*

- What is the church? • What is the purpose of the church? • What work (ministries) should the church do? • What other names are given for "the church"? • What are the qualifications for the church's leaders? • What is the church? • What is the purpose of the church? • What work (ministries) should the church do? • What other names are given for "the church"? • What are the qualifications for the church's leaders? • What is the church? • What is the purpose of the church? • What work (ministries) should the church do? • What other names are given

# The Church
## *Ecclesiology*

• What is the church? • What is the purpose of the church? • What work (ministries) should the church do? • What other names are given for "the church"? • What are the qualifications

for the church's leaders? • What is the church? • What is the purpose of the church? • What work (ministries) should the church do? • What other names are given

for "the church"? • What are the qualifications for the church's leaders? • What is the church? • What is the purpose of the church? • What work (ministries) should the church do?

# Future Events
## *Eschatology*

- What future events will involve Jesus Christ and what will happen?

- What future events will involve the church and what will happen?

- What future events will involve the angels and what will they do?

- What will happen to demons and Satan?

- What will happen to those who are not saved?

- Describe Heaven.

- Describe Hell and the Lake of Fire.

# Future Events
## *Eschatology*

- What future events will involve Jesus Christ and what will happen? • What future events will involve the church and what will happen? • What future events will involve the angels and what will they do? • What will happen to demons and Satan? • What will happen to those who are not saved? • Describe Heaven. • Describe Hell and the Lake of Fire.

# Future Events
## *Eschatology*

- What future events will involve Jesus Christ and what will happen?
- What future events will involve the church and what will happen?
- What future events will involve the angels and what will they do?
- What will happen to demons and Satan?
- What will happen to those who are not saved?
- Describe Heaven.
- Describe Hell and the Lake of Fire.
- What future events will involve Jesus Christ and what will happen?
- What future events will involve the church and what will happen?
- What will happen to demons and Satan?

# Future Events
## *Eschatology*

- What future events will involve Jesus Christ and what will happen? • What future events will involve the church and what will happen? • What future events will involve the angels and what will they do? • What will happen to demons and Satan? • What will happen to those who are not saved? • Describe Heaven. • Describe Hell and the Lake of Fire. • What future events will involve Jesus Christ and what will happen? • What future events will involve the church and what will happen? • What will happen to demons and Satan?

# Future Events
## Eschatology

- What future events will involve Jesus Christ and what will happen? • What future events will involve the church and what will happen? • What future events will involve the angels and what will they do? • What will happen to demons and Satan? • What will happen to those who are not saved? • Describe Heaven. • Describe Hell and the Lake of Fire. • What future events will involve Jesus Christ and what will happen? • What future events will involve the church and what will happen? • What will happen to demons and Satan?

# Future Events
## *Eschatology*

- What future events will involve Jesus Christ and what will happen? • What future events will involve the church and what will happen? • What future events will involve the angels and what will they do? • What will happen to demons and Satan? • What will happen to those who are not saved? • Describe Heaven. • Describe Hell and the Lake of Fire. • What future events will involve Jesus Christ and what will happen? • What future events will involve the church and what will happen? • What will happen to demons and Satan?

# Future Events
## *Eschatology*

• What future events will involve Jesus Christ and what will happen? • What future events will involve the church and what will happen? • What future events will involve the angels and what will they do? • What will happen to demons and Satan? • What will happen to those who are not saved? • Describe Heaven. • Describe Hell and the Lake of Fire. • What future events will involve Jesus Christ and what will happen? • What future events will involve the church and what will happen? • What will happen to demons and Satan?

# Future Events
## *Eschatology*

- What future events will involve Jesus Christ and what will happen? • What future events will involve the church and what will happen? • What future events will involve the angels and what will they do? • What will happen to demons and Satan? • What will happen to those who are not saved? • Describe Heaven. • Describe Hell and the Lake of Fire. • What future events will involve Jesus Christ and what will happen? • What future events will involve the church and what will happen? • What will happen to demons and Satan?

# Future Events
## *Eschatology*

- What future events will involve Jesus Christ and what will happen?
- What future events will involve the church and what will happen?
- What future events will involve the angels and what will they do?
- What will happen to demons and Satan?
- What will happen to those who are not saved?
- Describe Heaven.
- Describe Hell and the Lake of Fire.
- What future events will involve Jesus Christ and what will happen?
- What future events will involve the church and what will happen?
- What will happen to demons and Satan?

# Future Events
## *Eschatology*

- What future events will involve Jesus Christ and what will happen?
- What future events will involve the church and what will happen?
- What future events will involve the angels and what will they do?
- What will happen to demons and Satan?
- What will happen to those who are not saved?
- Describe Heaven.
- Describe Hell and the Lake of Fire.

# Future Events
## Eschatology

- What future events will involve Jesus Christ and what will happen?
- What future events will involve the church and what will happen?
- What future events will involve the angels and what will they do?
- What will happen to demons and Satan?
- What will happen to those who are not saved?
- Describe Heaven.
- Describe Hell and the Lake of Fire.
- What future events will involve Jesus Christ and what will happen?
- What future events will involve the church and what will happen?
- What will happen to demons and Satan?

*www.SimplyCharlotteMason.com*